NAME _____

All for STRINGS

THEORY WORKBOOK 1
by Gerald E. Anderson and Robert S. Frost

D0752126

Dear String Student:
Welcome to **ALL FOR STRINGS-THEORY WORKBOOK 1!**

THEORY WORKBOOK 1 will help you to understand the fundamentals and theory of music. The study of music fundamentals and theory together with careful practice in playing your instrument will help you to develop into a complete musician with the ability to perform with musical understanding.

Best Wishes!

Gerald E. Anderson
Robert S. Frost

ISBN 0-8497-3246-8

© **1988 NEIL A. KJOS MUSIC COMPANY,** 4382 Jutland Drive, San Diego, California
International copyright secured. All rights reserved. Printed in U.S.A.

 NEIL A. KJOS MUSIC COMPANY • SAN DIEGO, CALIFORNIA

1. DRAW CLEF SIGNS

The treble clef is also known as the G clef because the big loop circles the G line. Draw 12 treble clefs on the staff below. Use the examples as models.

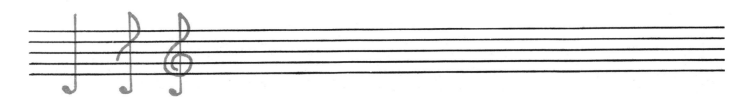

2. NUMBER LINES AND SPACES

The lines and spaces of the staff are always counted from the bottom to the top.
①On the staff below, number the lines from the bottom to the top with the numbers 1, 2, 3, 4, 5.
②On the staff below, number the spaces from the bottom to the top with the numbers 1, 2, 3, 4.

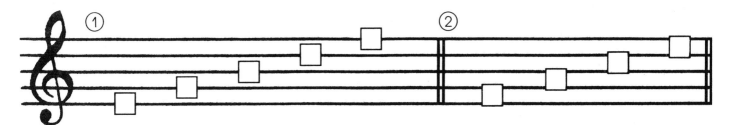

3. NAME LINES AND SPACES GOING UP

The musical alphabet uses the letters A B C D E F G.
Going from low to high on the staff, the names of the lines and spaces use the musical alphabet in order from A to G.
Name each line or space in the boxes provided. Refer to the musical alphabet.

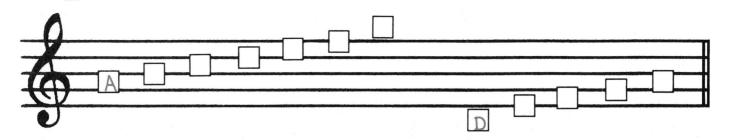

4. NAME LINES AND SPACES GOING DOWN

Going from high to low on the staff, the names of the lines and spaces use the musical alphabet in reverse (backwards) order: G F E D C B A.
Name each line or space in the boxes provided. Refer to the reverse order musical alphabet.

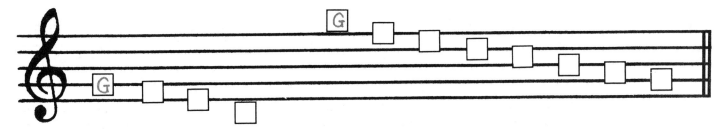

5. NAME LINES AND SPACES

Name each line or space in the box provided.

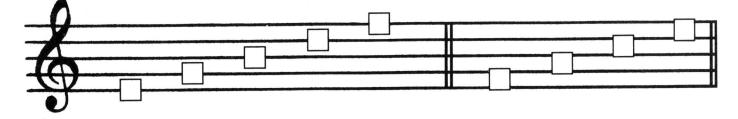

6. NAME NOTES

Write the name of each note on the blank provided.

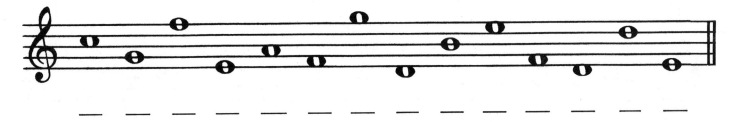

7. DRAW STEMS

Notes that are on lines or spaces below the third line have stems pointing up: ♩♩. Notes that are on the third line and above have stems pointing down: ♩♩. Draw stems on each of the notes below. Be sure each stem points in the correct direction.

8. DRAW HALF NOTES

The notehead of a half note is drawn like an oval as shown below. Draw half notes on every line and space of the staff. Use the examples as models. Be sure each stem points in the correct direction.

9. DRAW QUARTER NOTES

Quarter notes are drawn like half notes except the noteheads are filled in to make a solid notehead. Draw quarter notes on every line and space of the staff below. Use the examples as models.

10. DRAW HALF RESTS AND WHOLE RESTS

Half rests are small rectangles filled in and placed above the third line of the staff. Whole rests are placed below the fourth line. Draw half rests and whole rests on the staff below. Use the examples as models.

11. NAME NOTES

Write the name of each note on the blank line provided below each note.

12. DRAW BAR LINES/WRITE COUNTING

Draw bar lines for the two lines of music below so that each measure contains the correct number of beats. Write the counting on the blanks provided.

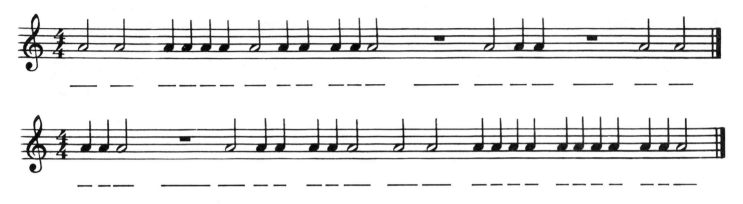

13. MATCHING

Match the correct term to each symbol. Write the number of the corresponding term in the box by the symbol.

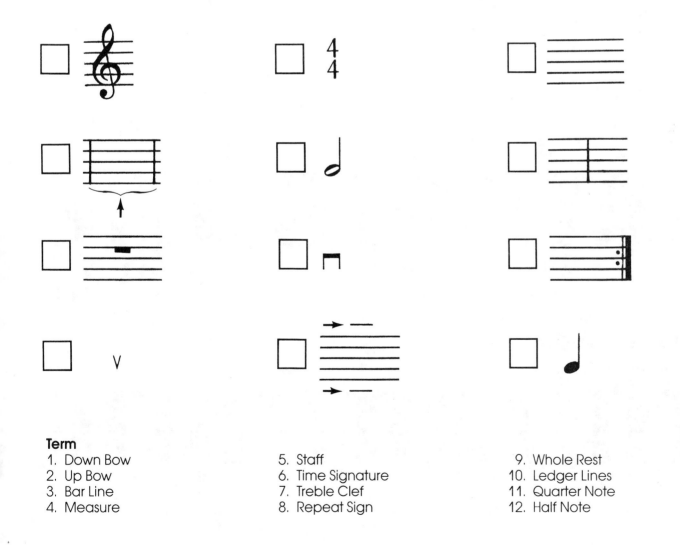

Term

1. Down Bow
2. Up Bow
3. Bar Line
4. Measure

5. Staff
6. Time Signature
7. Treble Clef
8. Repeat Sign

9. Whole Rest
10. Ledger Lines
11. Quarter Note
12. Half Note

14. LEARN THE KEYBOARD

All musicians need to know the piano keyboard. Each white key on the keyboard is named with a letter of the musical alphabet: A B C D E F G. Write the name of each white key on the keyboard below with the correct letter name. Up is to the right. Down is to the left.

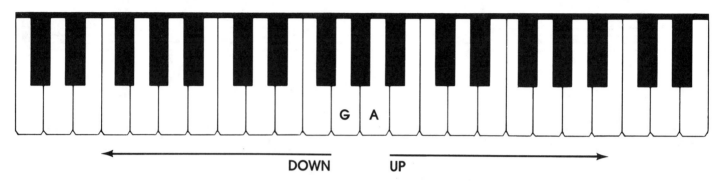

15. MARK C's AND F's

Write a C on all the C's and a F on all the F's on the keyboard below.

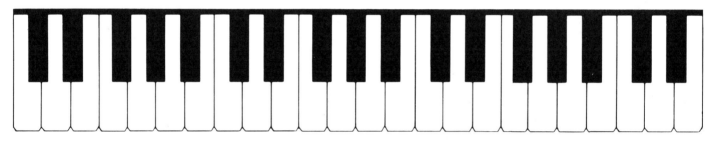

16. MARK B's AND E's

Write a B on all the B's and an E on all the E's on the keyboard below.

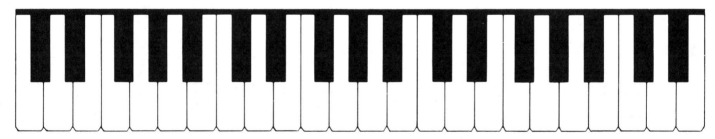

17. MARK A's, D's AND G's

Write an A on all the A's, a G on all the G's and a D on all the D's on the keyboard below.

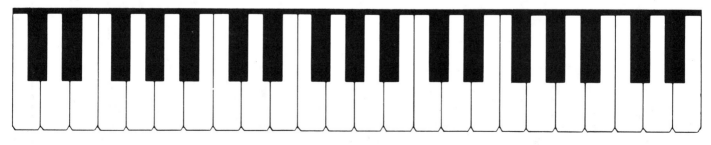

18. NAME NOTES

Write the name of each note on the blank provided.

___ ___ | ___ | ___ ___ ___ | ___ ___ | ___ ___ ___ | ___ ___ ‖

19. DRAW NOTES

Draw the notes on the staff as requested. Be sure each measure has the correct number of beats.

D   E | F♯ A E | F♯ D E D | A   E | D   E   G | F♯ D ‖

20. MUSICAL MATH

Fill in each blank with the number that solves each musical math problem.

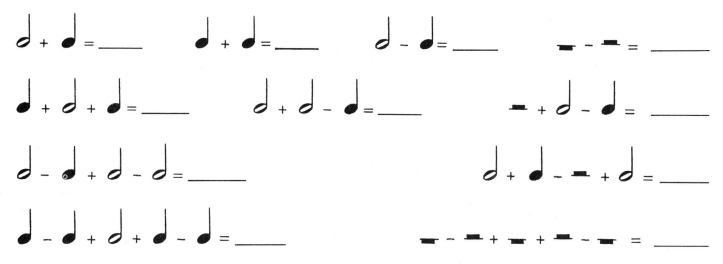

21. KEYBOARD/LEARN MIDDLE C

Middle C is found in the middle of the keyboard. In written music, using the treble clef, it is shown on the 1st ledger line below the staff. The examples below show the relationship of Middle C to the violin open strings on the staff and the keyboard.

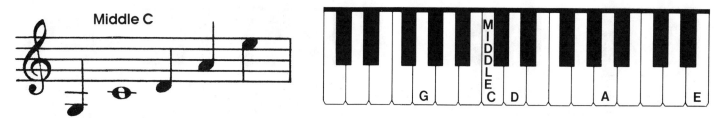

22. FINGERING CHART

Write the name of the note that is played at the place of each circle and square on the fingering chart below.

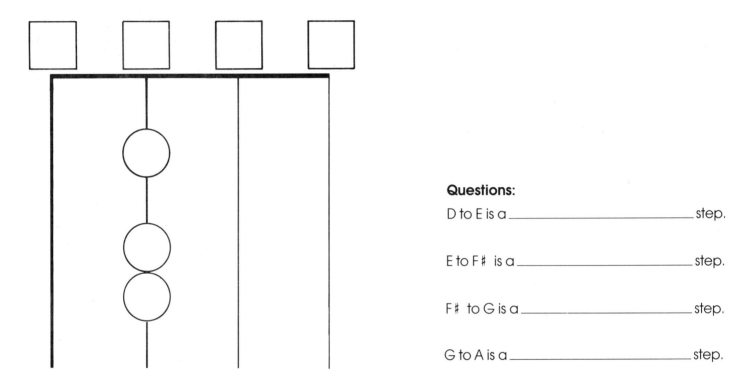

Questions:

D to E is a _____ step.

E to F♯ is a _____ step.

F♯ to G is a _____ step.

G to A is a _____ step.

23. NAME NOTES/DRAW NOTES

①Write the name of each note on the blank provided. ②Draw the notes from the fingering chart on the staff as requested. Use quarter notes. Be sure each stem points in the correct direction.

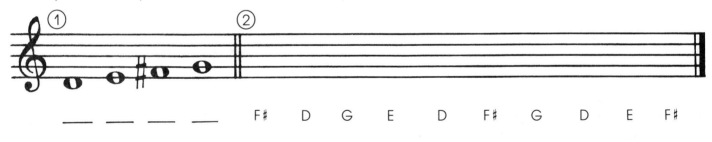

___ ___ ___ ___ ___   F♯   D   G   E   D   F♯   G   D   E   F♯

24. KEYBOARD/LEARN HALF STEPS AND WHOLE STEPS

A half step is the distance from one key to the nearest key with no key in between.

A whole step is made up of two half steps. It is the distance from one key to another with one key in between.

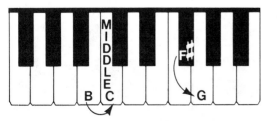 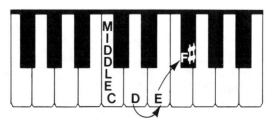

84VN

25. KEYBOARD STUDY

Write the letters on the keys for all notes shown in the fingering chart on page 8. Show proper relationship to middle C.

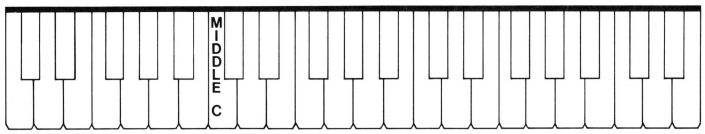

26. NAME NOTES

Write the name of each note on the blank provided.

27. DRAW A CLEF, TIME SIGNATURE AND NOTES

Draw your clef, a time signature and the notes requested. Be sure each measure has the correct number of beats.

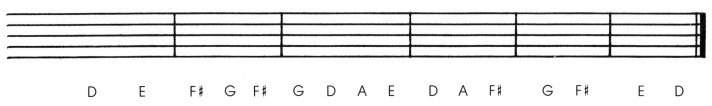

D   E   F♯   G F♯   G   D   A   E   D   A   F♯   G   F♯   E   D

28. NAME NOTES

Write the name of each note on the blank provided. Each measure will spell a familiar word.

29. DRAW QUARTER RESTS

Draw 12 quarter rests on the staff below. Begin by tracing the example below and then use the model to draw 12 more.

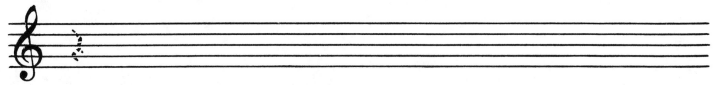

30. DRAW BAR LINES/WRITE COUNTING

Draw bar lines for the two lines of music below so that each measure contains the correct number of beats. Write the counting on the blanks provided.

31. MUSICAL MATH

Fill in each blank square with one note/rest to equal the total shown.

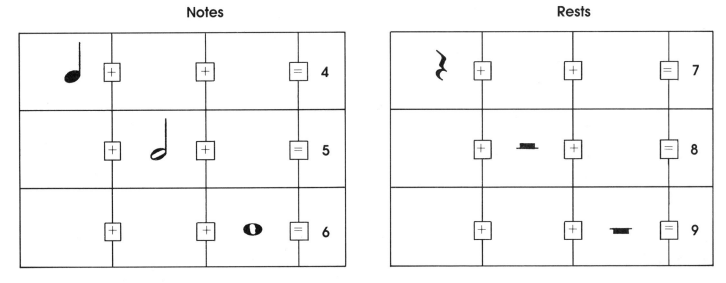

32. BALANCE THE SCALE

Write in ONE note or rest to balance each scale. Be sure that the notes or rests on one side of the scale balance the note or rest that you have written.

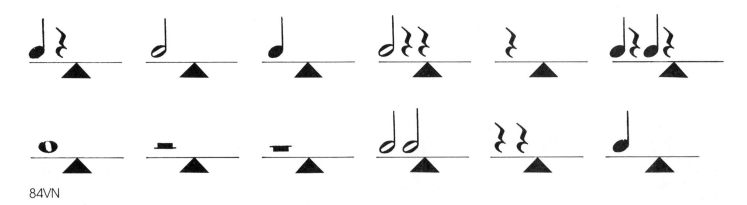

33. DRAW A KEY SIGNATURE

In measure 1, trace the sharps of the D Major key signature. In measures 2, 3, 4 and 5, write your clef and the key signature for D Major.

34. LEARN ABOUT TETRACHORDS

A tetrachord is a four note scale. A major tetrachord has a ½ step between the 3rd and 4th notes and forms the first four or last four notes of a major scale. The example below shows major tetrachords beginning on the open D and A string.

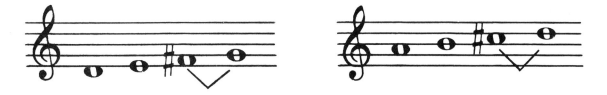

35. LEARN ABOUT MAJOR SCALES

A major scale is built by joining two major tetrachords. Therefore, a major scale has half steps between the third and fourth notes and the seventh and eighth notes. Circle each major tetrachord on the scale below.

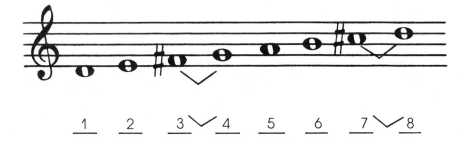

36. DRAW A CLEF, TIME SIGNATURE AND NOTES

Draw your clef, a time signature and the notes as requested. Be sure each measure has the correct number of beats.

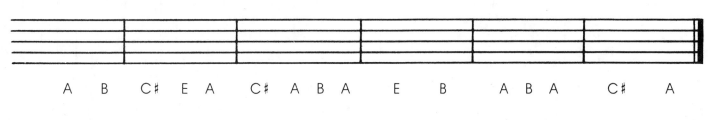

A   B   C♯ E A   C♯ A B A   E   B   A B A   C♯   A

37. FINGERING CHART

Write the name of the note that is played at the place of each circle on the fingering chart below. Place the sharps from the diagram on the staff to form the key signature of D Major.

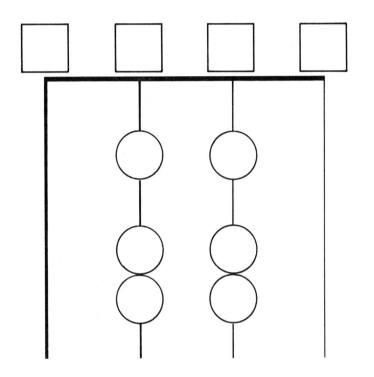

Questions:

The key of D Major has _____sharps.

The first sharp is _____

The second sharp is _____

E to F♯ is a _____step.

F♯ to G is a _____step.

B to C♯ is a _____step.

C♯ to D is a _____step.

38. NAME NOTES/DRAW NOTES

①Write the name of each note on the blank provided.   ②Draw the notes found in a D major scale on the staff as requested. Use quarter and half notes. Be sure each stem points in the correct direction.

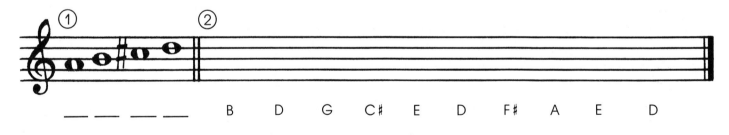

___ ___ ___ ___   B   D   G   C♯   E   D   F♯   A   E   D

39. KEYBOARD STUDY

Write the letters on the keys for the D Major scale. Show proper relationship to middle C.

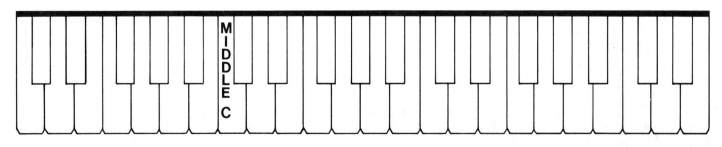

40. MUSICAL CROSSWORD PUZZLE

Write the name of each note in the correct box.

ACROSS

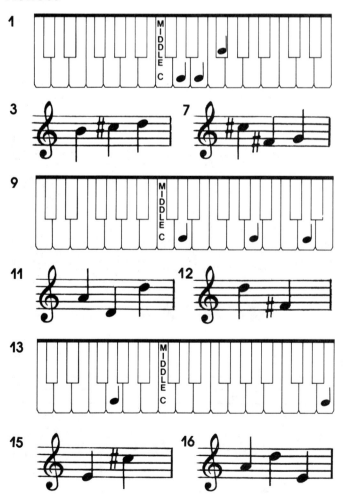

DOWN

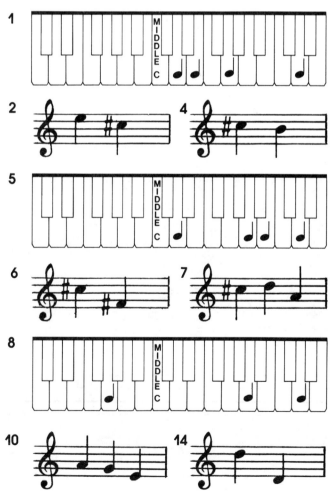

41. DRAW BAR LINES/WRITE COUNTING

Draw bar lines for the two lines of music below so that each measure contains the correct number of beats. Write the counting on the blanks provided.

42. MUSICAL MATH

Fill in each blank with the number that solves each musical math problem.

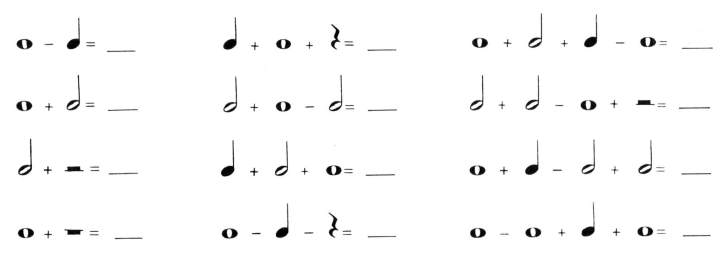

43. LEARN ABOUT MUSICAL PHRASES

A phrase is a short musical idea much like part of a sentence. Phrases are usually written in groups of four or eight measures. Some phrases have the feeling of completion like coming to the end of a sentence and others do not. Phrases are combined and often repeated to make the music sound complete or final.

44. COMPOSE MUSIC

Draw your clef, a time signature and a key signature. Write two four measure phrases using notes, rhythms and rests you have learned.

45. DRAW BAR LINES/WRITE COUNTING

Draw bar lines for the two lines of music below so that each measure contains the correct number of beats. Write the counting on the blanks provided.

46. MUSICAL MATH

Fill in each blank with the number that solves each musical math problem.

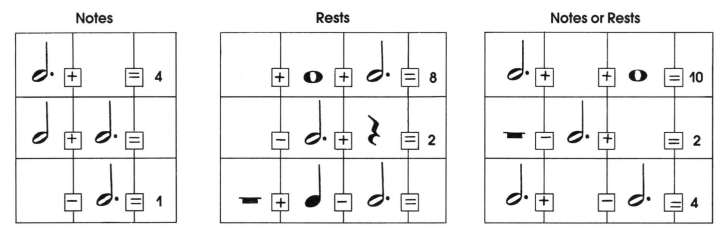

47. MUSICAL ROAD SIGNS

Every measure has a number. Answer each question by putting the correct measure number on the blank.

Questions:
Which measure would you play after measure 4? _____
Which measure would you play after measure 8? _____
Which measure would you play last? _____

48. IDENTIFY SLURS AND TIES

Write a **T** under all the ties and a **S** under all the slurs.

49. COMPLETE THE MEASURE

Complete each measure with ONE note or rest.

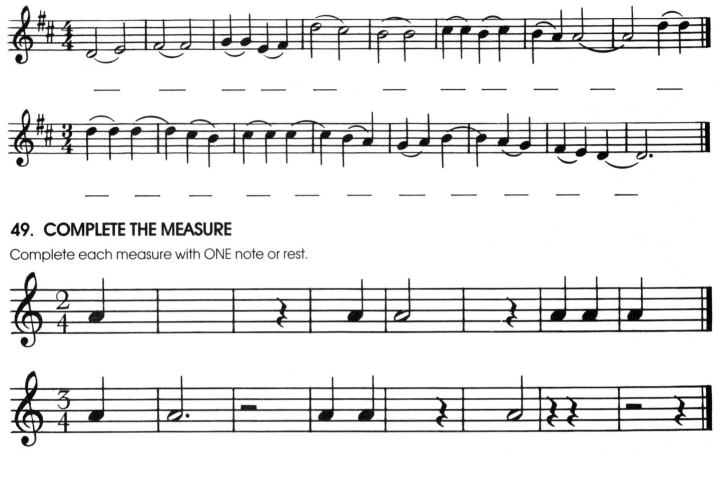

50. BALANCE THE SCALE

Write ONE note to balance each scale.

51. DRAW BAR LINES/WRITE COUNTING

Draw bar lines for the two lines of music below so that each measure contains the correct number of beats.
Write the counting on the blanks provided.

52. NAME NOTES

1. Write the name of the note that is played at the place of each circle and square on the fingering chart. These notes form the D arpeggio.
2. The notes on the staff below are in the D arpeggio. Write the name of each note on the blank provided.

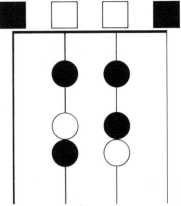

53. MATCHING

Match the correct name to each symbol. Write the number of the name in the box by the symbol.

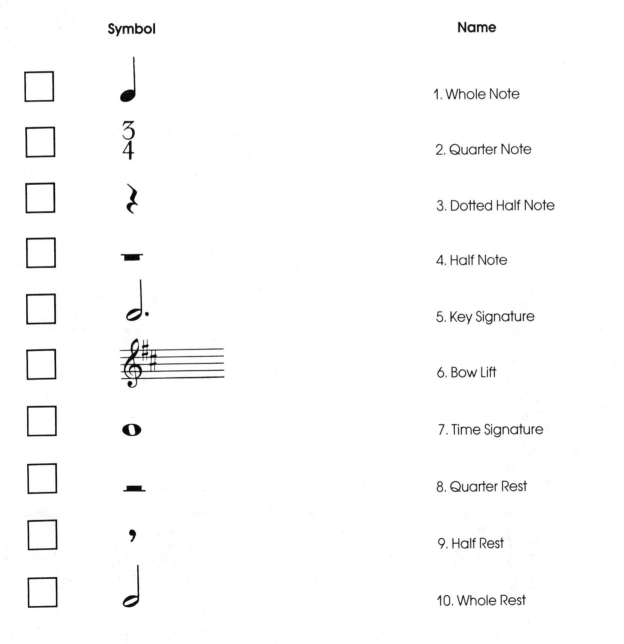

Symbol	Name
☐ ♩	1. Whole Note
☐ 3/4	2. Quarter Note
☐ 𝄽	3. Dotted Half Note
☐ ▬	4. Half Note
☐ 𝅗𝅥.	5. Key Signature
☐ (treble clef with 2 sharps)	6. Bow Lift
☐ 𝅝	7. Time Signature
☐ ▬	8. Quarter Rest
☐ '	9. Half Rest
☐ 𝅗𝅥	10. Whole Rest

54. FINGERING CHART

Write the name of the note that is played at the place of each circle and square on the fingering chart below. Place the sharps from the diagram on the staff to form the key signature for G Major.

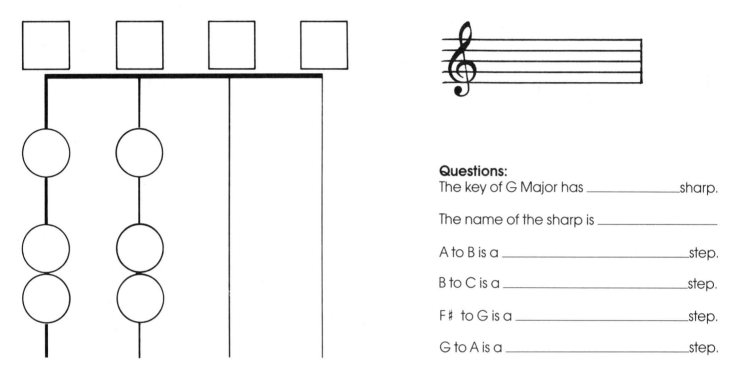

Questions:

The key of G Major has _____ sharp.

The name of the sharp is _____

A to B is a _____ step.

B to C is a _____ step.

F♯ to G is a _____ step.

G to A is a _____ step.

55. NAME NOTES/DRAW NOTES

① Write the name of each note on the blank provided.
② Draw the notes found in a G Major scale on the staff as requested. Use half notes. Be sure each stem points in the correct direction.

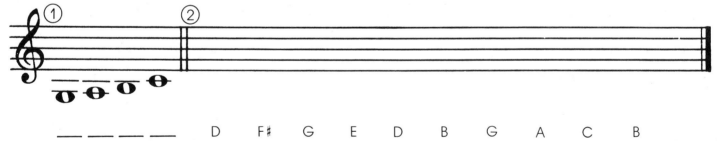

_____ _____ _____ _____ _____   D   F♯   G   E   D   B   G   A   C   B

56. KEYBOARD STUDY

Write the letters on the keys for the G Major scale. Show the proper relationship to middle C.

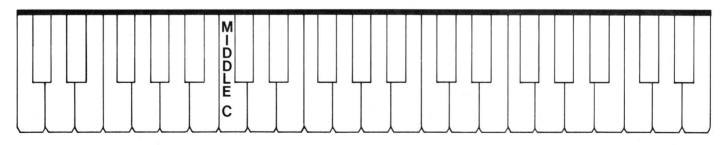

57. NAME NOTES

Write the name of each note on the blank provided.

____ ____ ____ ____ ____ ____ ____ ____ ____ ____

58. DRAW AND NAME MAJOR TETRACHORDS

Draw the notes found in the G, D and A Major tetrachord. Use whole notes. Write the name of the notes on the blanks provided.

____ ____ ____ ____ ____ ____ ____ ____ ____ ____ ____ ____

59. NAME NOTES

Write the name of each note on the blank provided.

____ ____ ____ ____ ____ ____ ____ ____ ____ ____ ____ ____

60. MUSICAL ROAD SIGNS

Every measure has a number. Answer each question by putting the correct measure number on the blank.

Questions:

Which measure would you play after measure 6? 1st time _____ 2nd time _____
Which measure would you play after measure 8? _____ measure 10? _____
Which measure would you play after measure 18? _____ measure 6—last time? _____

61. DRAW BAR LINES/WRITE COUNTING

Draw the bar lines for the two lines of music below so that each measure contains the correct number of beats. Write the counting on the blank provided.

62. BALANCE THE SCALE

Write notes or rests to balance each scale. Be sure that the notes or rests on one side of the scale balances the notes or rests that you have written.

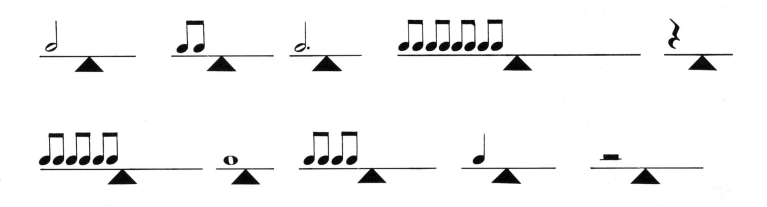

63. NAME NOTES

1. Write the name of the note that is played at the place of each circle on the fingering chart. Each note is played with a high second finger.
2. The notes on the staff below are played with a high second finger. Write the name of each note on the blank provided.

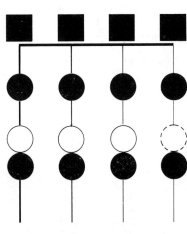

64. MATCHING

Match each word to the proper definition. Write the number of the word on the blank provided.

Word

1. Fermata
2. Andante
3. Slur
4. Moderato
5. Fine
6. Tonic
7. Arpeggio
8. Tie
9. Pick-up Notes
10. Allegro
11. Dominant
12. Ritard.

Definition

_____the first note of a scale

_____play the note longer than written

_____a curved line that connects two notes of the same pitch.

_____quick and lively

_____gradually slow the tempo

_____the notes of a chord played one at a time

_____moderate speed

_____the fifth note of the scale

_____a curved line that connects two or more notes of different pitches

_____moderately slow

_____notes that come before the first full measure of music

_____a word that means the end

65. LEARN MINOR TETRACHORDS

A minor tetrachord has a ½ step between the 2nd and 3rd notes and forms the first four notes of a minor scale. The example below shows minor tetrachords beginning on the open D and A string.

66. DRAW NATURAL AND SHARP SIGNS

①Trace then draw several natural signs.
②Add natural and sharp signs to the notes on the staff as requested. Place the natural or sharp sign to the left and on the same space or line as the notehead.

67. FINGERING CHART

Write the name of the note that is played at the place of each circle and square on the fingering chart below.

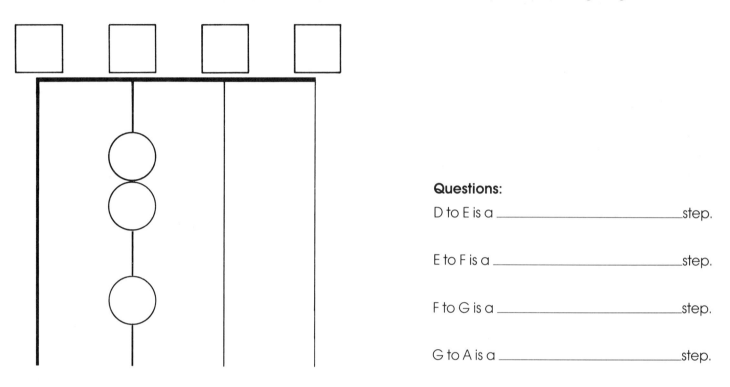

Questions:

D to E is a _____step.

E to F is a _____step.

F to G is a _____step.

G to A is a _____step.

68. NAME NOTES/DRAW NOTES

①Write the name of each note on the blank provided
②Draw the notes on the staff as requested. Use dotted half notes. Be sure each stem points in the correct direction.

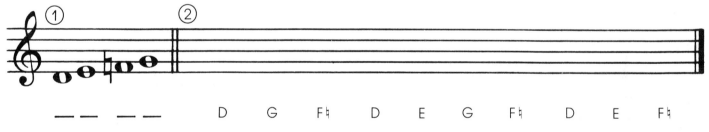

___ ___ ___ ___ ___   D   G   F♮   D   E   G   F♮   D   E   F♮

69. KEYBOARD STUDY

Write the letters on the keys for all the notes shown in the fingering chart above. Show proper relationship to middle C.

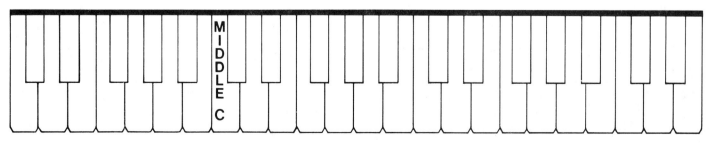

70. FINGERING CHART

Write the name of the note that is played at the place of each circle and square on the fingering chart below.

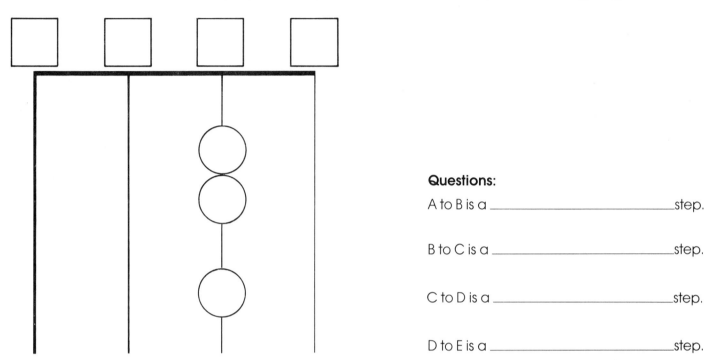

Questions:

A to B is a _____step.

B to C is a _____step.

C to D is a _____step.

D to E is a _____step.

71. NAME NOTES/DRAW NOTES

① Write the name of each note on the blank provided.
② Draw the new notes on the staff as requested. Use quarter and half notes. Be sure each stem points in the correct direction.

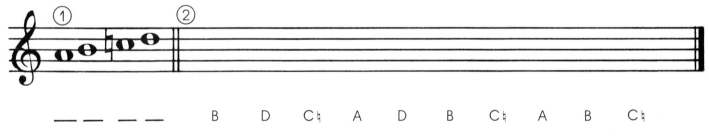

72. KEYBOARD STUDY

Write the letters on the keys for all the notes shown in the fingering chart above. Show proper relationship to middle C.

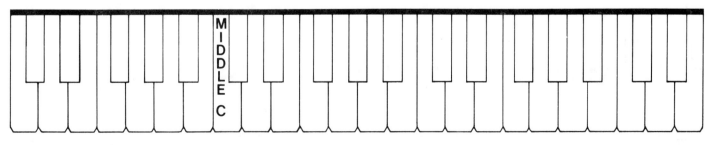

73. IDENTIFY DYNAMICS

Write the word, symbol or meaning of each dynamic in the box provided.

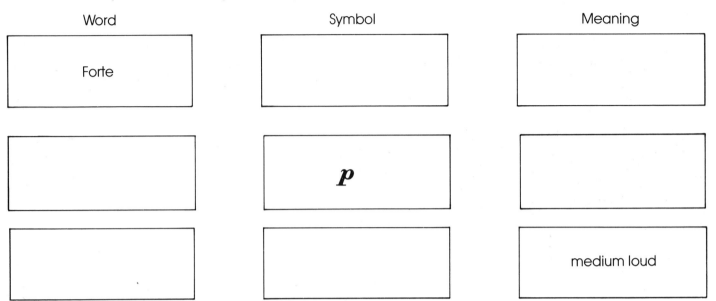

Word	Symbol	Meaning
Forte		
	p	
		medium loud

74. IDENTIFY HIGH AND LOW NOTES

Identify the fingering for each of the notes as follows: On the blanks provided, place an **H** for notes played with a high second finger and a **L** for notes played with a low second finger.

75. MUSICAL MATH

Fill in each blank square with one note or rest to solve each musical problem.

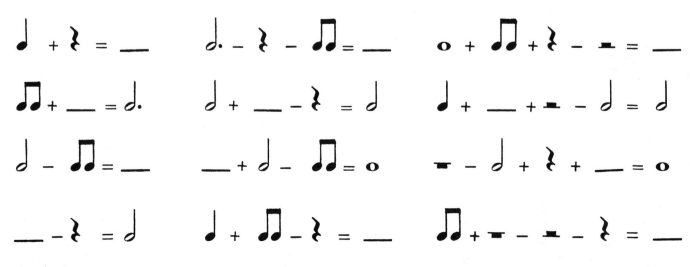

76. FINGERING CHART

Write the name of the note that is played at the place of each circle and square on the fingering chart below.

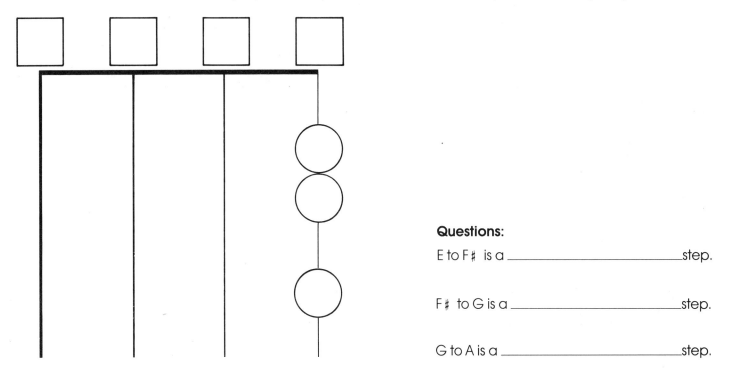

Questions:

E to F♯ is a _____ step.

F♯ to G is a _____ step.

G to A is a _____ step.

77. NAME NOTES/DRAW NOTES

① Write the name of each note on the blank provided.
② Draw the new notes on the staff as requested. Use whole and half notes. Be sure each stem points in the correct direction.

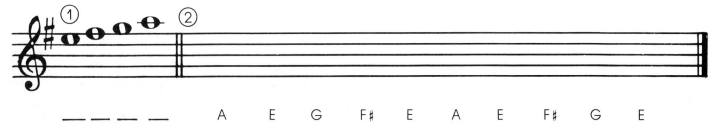

___ ___ ___ ___ ___   A   E   G   F♯   E   A   E   F♯   G   E

78. KEYBOARD STUDY

Write the letters on the keys for all the notes shown in the fingering chart above. Show proper relationship to middle C.

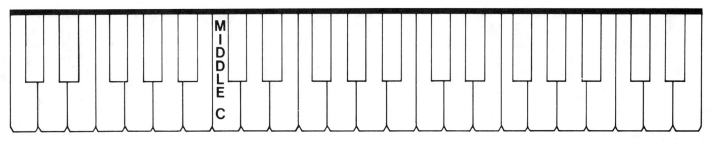

79. FINGERING CHART

Write the name of the note that is played at the place of each circle and square on the fingering chart below. Write the key signature for C Major on the staff below.

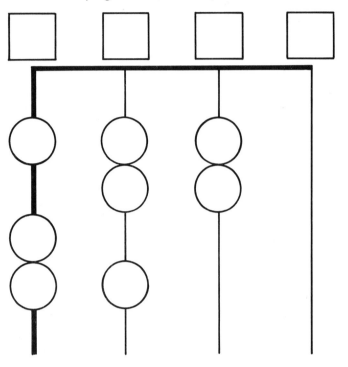

Questions:

The key of C Major has _____ sharps.

D to E is a _____ step.

E to F is a _____ step.

A to B is a _____ step.

B to C is a _____ step.

80. NAME NOTES/DRAW NOTES

① Write the name of each note on the blank provided.
② Draw the notes found in a C major scale on the staff as requested. Use quarter notes. Be sure each stem points in the correct direction.

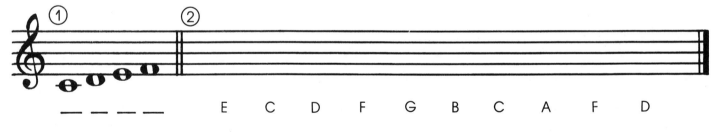

_ _ _ _   E   C   D   F   G   B   C   A   F   D

81. KEYBOARD STUDY

Write the letters on the keys for the notes of the C Major scale. Show proper relationship to middle C.

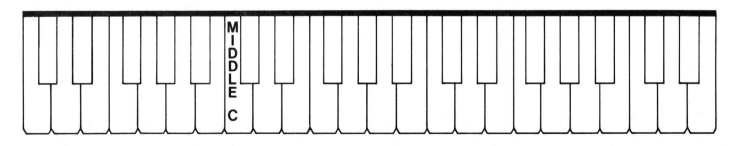

82. NAME NOTES

1. Write the name of the note that is played at the place of each circle on the fingering chart. Each note is played with a low second finger.
2. The notes on the staff below are played with a low second finger. Write the name of each note on the blank provided.

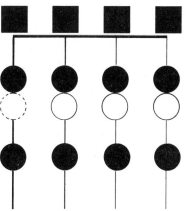

___   ___   ___   ___   ___   ___   ___   ___

83. NAME AND DRAW ARPEGGIOS

Name the notes in the C, D and G arpeggios on the blanks provided. Draw all the notes of the C, D and G arpeggios that you have learned. Use quarter notes. Be sure each stem points in the correct direction.

_C_ ___ ___ ___   _D_ ___ ___ ___   _G_ ___ ___ ___

84. DRAW AND NAME MAJOR AND MINOR TETRACHORDS

Draw the notes of the minor and major tetrachords as indicated. Name the notes of each tetrachord on the blanks provided. Use whole notes.

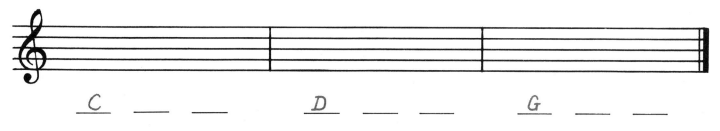

___ ___ ___ ___   ___ ___ ___ ___   ___ ___ ___ ___   ___ ___ ___ ___

85. MUSICAL MATH

Solve each musical problem by placing the correct answer (number) above each division line.

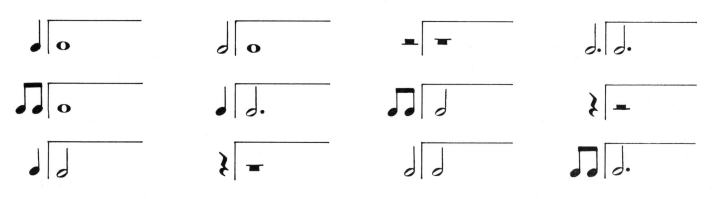

84VN

86. DRAW MUSICAL SYMBOLS

Draw the following musical symbols in the boxes.

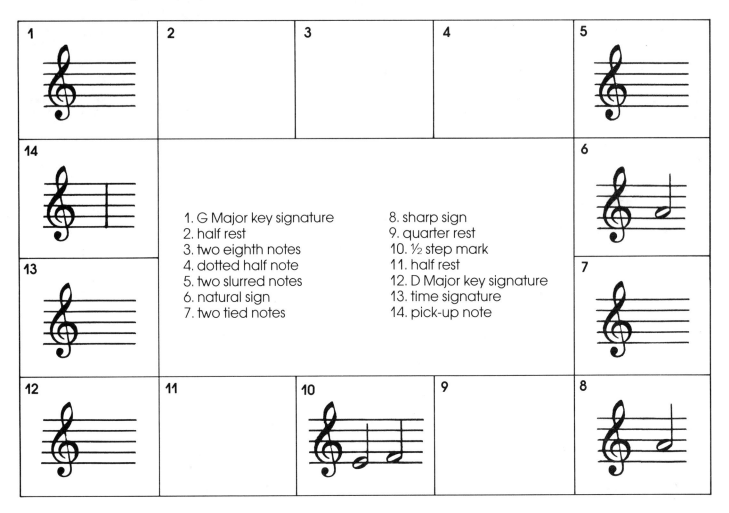

1. G Major key signature
2. half rest
3. two eighth notes
4. dotted half note
5. two slurred notes
6. natural sign
7. two tied notes

8. sharp sign
9. quarter rest
10. ½ step mark
11. half rest
12. D Major key signature
13. time signature
14. pick-up note

87. COMPOSE MUSIC

Draw your clef, a time signature and a key signature. Write in phrases using the notes, rhythms and rests you have learned.

88. FINGERING CHART

Write the name of the note that is played at the place of each circle and square on the fingering chart below. Place the sharps from the chart on the staff to form the correct key signature.

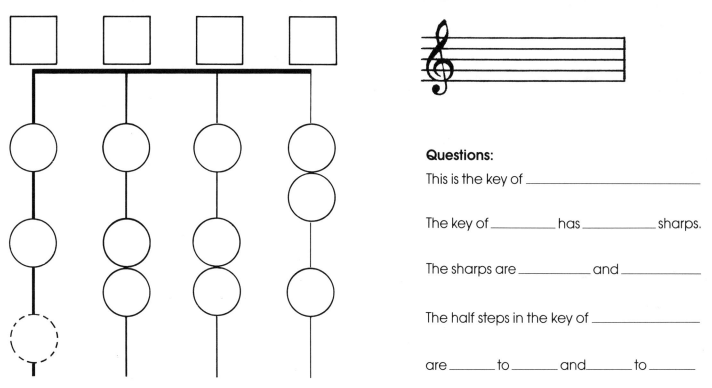

Questions:

This is the key of _____

The key of _____ has _____ sharps.

The sharps are _____ and _____

The half steps in the key of _____

are _____ to _____ and _____ to _____

89. DRAW NOTES/NAME NOTES

Draw a note on the staff for each note in the fingering chart above (low to high). Name the notes on the blanks provided, add the key signature and place half step markings where appropriate.

90. KEYBOARD STUDY

Write the letters on the keys for a one octave D Major scale. Show proper relationship to Middle C.

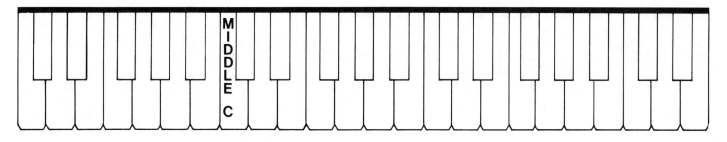

91. FINGERING CHART

Write the name of the note that is played at the place of each circle and square on the fingering chart below.
Place the sharps from the chart on the staff to form the correct key signature.

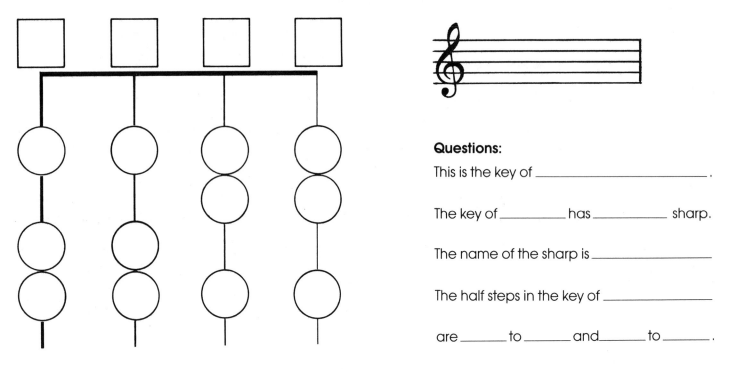

Questions:

This is the key of _____ .

The key of _____ has _____ sharp.

The name of the sharp is _____

The half steps in the key of _____

are _____ to _____ and_____ to _____ .

92. DRAW NOTES/NAME NOTES

Draw a note on the staff for each note in the fingering chart above (low to high). Name the notes on the
blanks provided, add the key signature and place half step markings where appropriate.

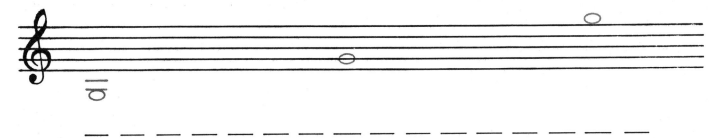

93. KEYBOARD STUDY

Write the letters on the keys for a two octave G Major scale. Show proper relationship to Middle C.

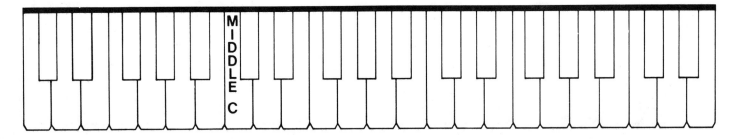

94. FINGERING CHART

Write the name of the note that is played at the place of each circle and square on the fingering chart below. Write the correct key signature.

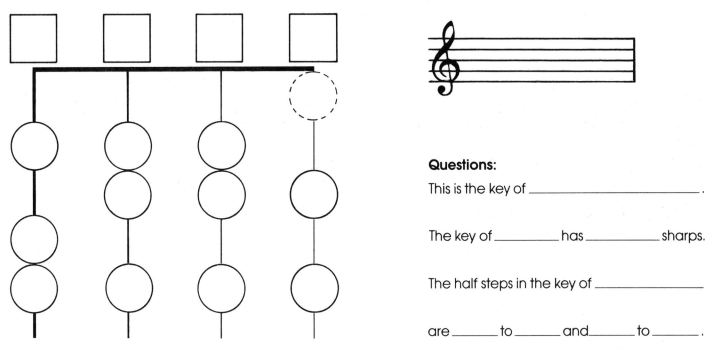

Questions:

This is the key of _____ .

The key of _____ has _____ sharps.

The half steps in the key of _____

are _____ to _____ and _____ to _____ .

95. DRAW NOTES/NAME NOTES

Draw a note on the staff for each note shown in the fingering chart above (low to high). Name the notes on the blanks provided, add the key signature and place half step markings where appropriate. Use whole notes.

96. KEYBOARD STUDY

Write the letters on the keys for a one octave C Major scale. Show proper relationship to middle C.

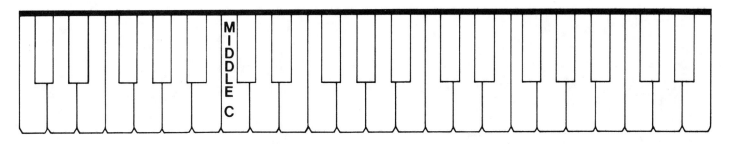

97. DEFINE TERMS AND SIGNS

Define the following or state what the word or sign wants you to do.

1. **Allegro** _____

2. **Andante** _____

3. Arco _____

4. ⊕ _____

5. *Da Capo* _____

6. *Dal Segno* _____

7. *Divisi* _____

8. Fermata _____

9. *Fine* _____

10. Forte _____

11. Louré _____

12. L.H. _____

13. Mezzo forte _____

14. **Moderato** _____

15. Natural _____

16. Piano _____

17. Pizzicato _____

18. *Ritard.* _____

19. Sharp _____

20. 𝄋 _____

21. Slur _____

22. Slurred staccato _____

23. Tie _____

24. U.H. _____

25. W.B. _____